Not What It Seems

Contents

Luiz and the Pink Dolphin

Written by Tom Pipher
Illustrated by Rick Youmans

Luiz lived with his mother in a hut on the Amazon River. His hut floated on big logs. When the river water went up, his hut went up, too.

Every day, Luiz went swimming in the river. Every day, he fished in the river. And, at night, as Luiz sat by his mother she would tell him stories about Bouto, the pink dolphin.

"In the river," said his mother, "there is a beautiful pink dolphin. She is called Bouto. By day, she swims between the trees of the underwater jungle. But by night, when the moon is bright, it is said that Bouto can turn herself into a beautiful woman."

"Like you, mother?" asked Luiz as he fell asleep.

The next day as Luiz was swimming in the river, he saw a splash. A beautiful pink dolphin jumped over him. It was Bouto. Luiz swam under the dolphin. They swam and played all day in the waters of the Amazon River.

That night, Luiz's mother told more stories of the beautiful pink dolphin. "Bouto can be a good friend for you, Luiz. She will keep the terrible piranha away. She will chase the tambaqui right to your hook. She might even find a pirarucu for you."

And Luiz fell asleep, dreaming of Bouto and all the fish he would catch.

What kinds of stories do you think Luiz's mother tells him? Can you make up a story about the pink dolphin and tell it to a friend?

The next day, Luiz fished all day long. No fat tambaqui came to his hook. No very large pirarucu came to his hook. Not even a little piranha came. And where was his friend, Bouto? Luiz sat in his boat. He was sad. As the sun went down, Luiz was just about ready to give up.
Then a very very large pirarucu took his hook.
The pirarucu pulled with all its might, and Luiz went flying out of the boat. As he fell into the underwater jungle of the Amazon, his head hit the side of the boat. All went black.

The splash told the piranhas that something good to eat was in the water. They came swimming... ten, twenty, thirty, forty, fifty hungry piranhas!

The splash sent a message to someone else, too. Just as the hungry piranhas came from their underwater jungle, so did Bouto. She took Luiz by the hand and pulled him away. She pulled him out of the underwater jungle. She pulled him to the bank of the Amazon River. She pulled Luiz to a safe place – away from the hungry piranhas.

7

Luiz woke up. It was good to breathe the air again. He looked up into the sunset sky. And there was his mother, holding his head in her lap. "Oh, Mother, so you are the beautiful woman in the story. You are Bouto!" said Luiz.

His mother just smiled.

Is Luiz's mother really the dolphin or is Luiz dreaming? What do you think?

Harley Pete

Written by
Peter Mair

Illustrated
by Kelvin
Hawley

Harley Pete had a motorbike
that was big and mean and fast.
And when he rode that motorbike.
he never came in last.

How do you think
Harley Pete got his
name?

Harley Pete had a motorbike
that had chrome along its pipes.
And vee twin motors down below.
and back and front bright lights.

Harley Pete had a motorbike
that made people stop to look.
It made a scary thundering sound.
and everything just shook.

Harley Pete had a motorbike
that zoomed and raced and sped.
And he loved that motorbike so much
he'd tuck it into bed.

What kind of person do
you think Harley Pete is?

So . . .
if Harley Pete comes down your street
with a frightening roar,
come up to him (with a great big grin).
Don't hide behind your door!

The Birdman

Written by Paul Reeder
Illustrated by Mark Wilson

An old, old man had moved into the
house at the end of Paul's street.
One day, Paul and his friend Shane
were walking home from school.
They walked past the old man's house.

"People say he doesn't like children,"
said Shane.

"Who doesn't like children?"
asked Paul.

"The birdman," answered Shane.
"People say he's crazy, because he lives
with lots of birds. That's why they call him
the birdman."

Just then, there was a very loud noise.
It got dark. Paul and Shane looked up.
Birds were everywhere, flying above
their heads.

"Run!" yelled Shane. "The birdman's
coming to get us!"

Paul stood and watched the birds.
They flew up and circled around and around
in the sky before flying into the trees.

"Wow! Have you ever seen so many birds?"
said Paul.

But Shane did not answer.
He was running for home.

"They're pigeons," said a voice.
"Homing pigeons."

Paul jumped. There was the birdman.

Paul wanted to run away, like Shane,
but he was too scared. His legs wobbled
and he fell down.

"Would you like to come and see my birds?"
asked the birdman.

"My dad says not to talk to strangers,"
answered Paul, and he turned and ran
all the way home.

That night, Paul dreamed about giant
pigeons flying about his bedroom.
The birdman, with his long bushy beard,
was flying around with them, too.

The next day, Paul found a book
about pigeons in the school library

"Pigeons can carry messages from one city
to another city," he said to Shane. "People
used pigeons in war time, too. They sent
messages. The messages were strapped
to the legs of pigeons.

"Sometimes, when a plane was shot down,
pigeons were sent back to the air base with
messages and a map. People knew, then,
where the plane had been shot down."

That day on the way home from school,
Paul stopped outside the birdman's house.
Some of the pigeons were sitting in the
trees. Paul thought about them carrying
messages all over the world.

**Why do you think Paul
wanted to learn more
about pigeons when he
was scared of the
birdman?**

When Paul got home, his dad said, "I met the birdman in town today. I gave him a ride home, and he left a package in the car. Could you take it up to him please, Paul?"

Paul was scared. What would he say? Was the birdman really crazy like people said? Paul liked the idea of getting a close look at the pigeons. He knew, too, that everything would be OK. His dad had asked him to go.

When Paul got to the birdman's house, he found the birdman with his pigeons. "You left a package in Dad's car," said Paul.

"Thank you," said the birdman. "Packages come home, just like my beautiful pigeons."

"I read about pigeons in a book at school," said Paul. "I read about how they can carry messages all over the world."

"These birds fly a long way," said the birdman, "but they always come home. Come and see me again. I will tell you more about my birds."

From that day on, Paul always stopped at the birdman's house on his way home from school. Each day, he helped the birdman look after the birds. Each day, the birdman told him more and more about his beautiful birds.

One day when Paul got to the birdman's house, he saw a note. The note said

*Please look after
my beautiful birds.
I am in the hospital.
See you soon.*

Each day on his way home from school, Paul went to the birdman's house and fed the pigeons.

Each night, Paul and his dad went to the hospital to see the birdman. He told the birdman how his beautiful birds were doing.

Some days, the birdman spoke to Paul. Other days, he was too weak, and he just looked at Paul.

One day, Paul took a special present to the birdman. It was a little pigeon that had been born while the birdman was in the hospital. Paul had looked after it each day. He was teaching it to fly home. Each day, he took it a bit farther away from the birdman's house. Each day, it flew home again. Paul opened the box for the birdman, and the little pigeon sat on the birdman's bed.

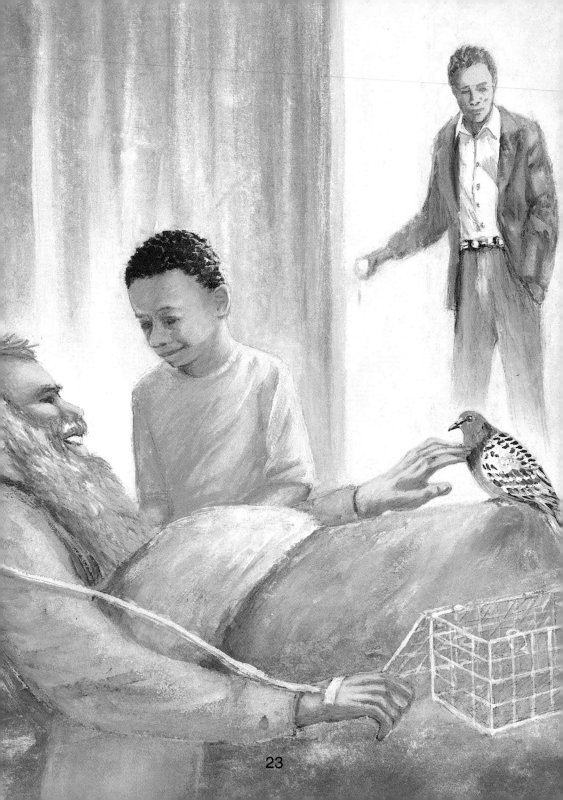

The next day, the birdman died. Paul was at school. He did not know that the birdman had died. After school, he went to the birdman's house to feed the pigeons. Sitting on the gate was the pigeon that Paul had taken to the birdman when he was in the hospital. It had a message tied to its leg. Paul opened up the message. It said,

Birds love to fly free.
Please look after my beautiful birds for me.
Don't let anyone put them in cages.
Take care, Paul, and thank you
for being my friend.

That night, Paul started teaching the pigeons to fly to his home.

What message did you get from reading this story?

24

The Eye in the Day Sky

Written by Dot Meharry
Illustrated by Kelvin Hawley

At the beginning of time, owls were day birds. Owls had big eyes that could see for a long way. Their sharp claws were always ready to catch the small animals of the earth. All day long, they would hunt for food. The small animals were never safe from the owls.

The small animals tried to hide in the trees, but the owls flew between the branches and snatched them up with their sharp claws. The small animals tried to hide in holes under the ground, but the owls waited for them to come out. They chased after them with their ready claws.

The small animals tried to hide in the darkness of the night. But the owls were so greedy that they began to hunt the small animals at night, too.

The small animals of the earth called out to the moon in the night sky to help them. "Oh, great Eye in the Night Sky, you can see what the greedy owls are doing. Please come down and help us."

But the great eye in the night sky said nothing.

So the small animals of the earth called out to the big yellow sun in the day sky.

"Oh, great Eye in the Day Sky, you can see what the greedy owls are doing. Please come down and help us."

The big yellow sun looked down at the small earth animals. "Meet me in the morning. Go to where the land meets the sky. Cover your faces. You cannot look at me, because I am too bright."

In the morning, the small animals of the earth went to where the land met the sky. They waited for the big yellow eye in the sky to come.

The greedy owls saw the small animals of the earth waiting where the land meets the sky. They swooped down to the small animals.

The small animals of the earth shook with fear. They were about to run away when the sun rose up. The small animals fell down to the ground and covered their eyes, just as the sun had told them to do.

But the greedy owls kept their big eyes wide open.
They flew into the sun. "Ahhhhh!" they screeched.

They turned away from the sun, but it was too late. The
sun had blinded their eyes. They could not see where they
were going. They could not see well enough to hunt the
small animals of the earth. The great eye in the day sky
looked down on the greedy owls. "Because you have been
so greedy, you will never be able to see in the day again.
You can only use your eyes at night. And you must hide
when you know I am coming." And the great eye in the day
sky went on its way.

WILDCATS

Leopard

Glossary

🐾 **Amazon** – a river in South America

🐾 **air base** – a place where military planes are stored and where they take off and land

🐾 **homing pigeons** – pigeons that are bred with an instinctive knowledge of how to fly home

🐾 **piranha** – small fish of South America with very strong jaws and sharp teeth that often attack other animals

🐾 **pirarucu** – a freshwater fish of South America

🐾 **tambaqui** – a freshwater fish of South America

🐾 **underwater jungle** – plant life that grows junglelike on the underwater floor of rivers and lakes